Let's Recycle!

by Dana Carroll

With the Editors of TIME For Kids

Table of Contents

Chapter I

Tons of Garbage

Every day we throw away things we don't want to use anymore. We throw away old newspapers, metal cans, plastic bottles, juice cartons, and glass jars.

The garbage we throw away may be taken to a garbage dump. Garbage takes up a lot of space. It is not a good use of our land.

Garbage dumps are ugly and smelly.

Landfills are better than dumps, but garbage is still a problem.

Garbage is also taken to a **sanitary landfill**. It is buried there. A landfill looks and smells better than a garbage dump. But it does not solve the problem: How can we get rid of a lot of trash?

Chapter 2

Reduce It and Reuse It

Everyone can help **reduce** the amount of garbage. We can buy products that last a long time. For example, paper cups are used once and thrown in the garbage. But drinking glasses can be used again and again.

We can **reuse** things made of paper, plastic, metal, and glass. We can find new ways to use them. We can use a glass jar as a flower vase. We can use a carton as a planter. An artist can even use old cans to make art!

Plastic milk jugs can be reused as planters.

Metal cans were reused to make this dinosaur model.

When people give away old things, it reduces garbage. There are places that take old furniture, clothes, and toys.

Clothing can be used again and again.

CLOTHING DRIVE

These places fix up old things so they are almost as good as new. Then these things are sold to other people and used again.

Chapter 3
Recycle It

Towns all over the United States are cutting down on waste. They reduce, reuse, and **recycle**, too. The people of California had a "Clean the Beach Day."

People enjoy a clean beach.

People picked up all the **litter** on the beach. They collected thousands of metal cans and plastic bottles for recycling. The people made their beaches beautiful and clean again.

Chapter 4

How Are Things Recycled?

When a town has a recycling plan, paper, metal, glass, and plastic are recycled. Each family or household sorts the items and places them in special bags or bins to be recycled.

Glass is recycled to make new glass. It is also used in paving roads. Paper is made into new paper and paper products. Recycling metal reduces air and water pollution. It saves **energy**, too.

This playground equipment was made from recycled plastic.

Ground-up glass for recycling

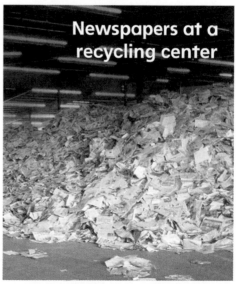

Newspapers at a recycling center

Chapter 5

How Can People Help?

Every state in the nation must take steps to reduce, reuse, and recycle.

Once a year Texas has a "Trash-Off Day." On this day, people collect litter from parks, roads, and neighborhoods.

Don't Mess with Texas
TR★SH-OFF

Kids pitch in on "Trash-Off Day."

People in many states get a deposit back when they recycle bottles and cans. But money is not the most important thing.

Earth's air, water, and land are much cleaner when we recycle.

Let's spread the word. Everyone can help to reduce, reuse, and recycle!

Glossary

 energy (EN-uhr-jee) power from electricity and other sources that makes machines work *(page 11)*

 litter (LIT-uhr) bits of trash scattered about in a messy way *(page 9)*

 recycle (ree-SIGH-kuhl) to use waste to make new things *(page 8)*

 reduce (ri-DEWS) to make smaller or use less of something *(page 4)*

 reuse (ree-YEWZ) to use something again *(page 5)*

 sanitary landfill (SAN-i-ter-ee LAND-fil) land that has been filled in by dumping garbage and mixing or covering it with soil *(page 3)*

Index